GOOD REASONS TO DIET
GOOD REASONS **NOT** TO DIET

Gladiola Montana

Illustrations by

Charles Goll

GIBBS·SMITH
P
PUBLISHER

SALT LAKE CITY

99 98 97   8 7 6 5 4 3 2 1

This is a Peregrine Smith Book, published by
Gibbs Smith, Publisher
P.O. Box 667
Layton, Utah 84041

Design by J. Scott Knudsen
Printed and bound in the U.S.A.

Library of Congress Cataloging-in-Publication
Data

Montana, Gladiola, 1949–
50 good reasons to diet/50 good reasons not to diet
/ Gladiola Montana : illustrated by Charles Goll.
—1st ed.
p.   cm.
ISBN 0-87905-786-6
1. Reducing diet—Humor.   I. Title.
PN6231.D64A15   1997
818'.5402—dc20   96-41238
                                CIP

50 Good Reasons *Not* to Diet

This book is dedicated to all that you and I have lost, year after year.

50 Good Reasons *Not* to Diet

50 Good Reasons *Not* to Diet

Not to Diet

diet is nothing more than a simple, slow trip to hell in a handbasket made of fat-free cottage cheese and sugarless pear halves.

A diet is nothing more than a simple lifestyle change.

Not to Diet

The more space you take up coming into a room,
the bigger the impression you make.

You notice that doorways are shrinking.

Not to Diet

If you've ever been in even the smallest collision, you know that good bumpers are essential to your survival.

To Diet

Your front end is on the march and your rear end
is getting further behind.

Not to Diet

ur mattress and favorite chair have been custom-fitted, just for you.

To Diet

Your mattress is sinking into a severe depression.

Not to Diet

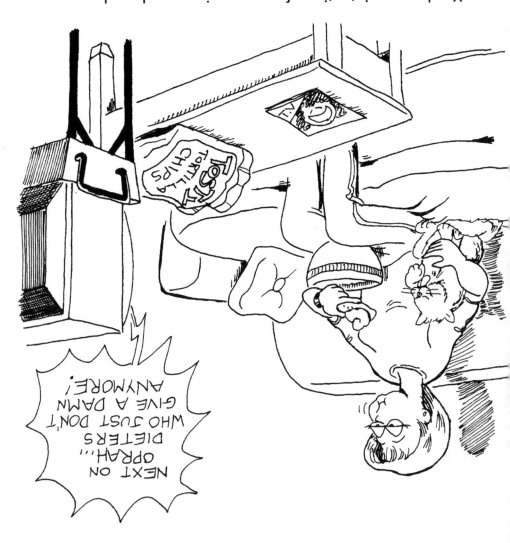

You have no intention of ever crossing your legs; how could you balance the bowl of salsa?

To Diet

You've never been in the army, but every time you cross your legs
you have to wage the battle of the bulge.

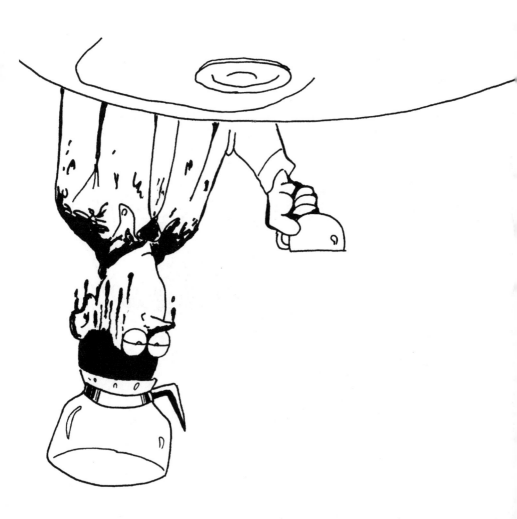

On a diet, the first thing you lose is your good nature.

To Diet

On a diet, you have nothing to lose but flab.

The refrigerator repairman is a studly hunk.

WE'VE BEEN NAUGHTY AGAIN, HAVEN'T WE?

To Diet

Your refrigerator door is on its fifth set of hinges.

Not to Diet

Get real. If you believe any fat-free food tastes great, you'd probably enjoy a bite or two out of the box it comes in, as well.

<u>To Diet</u>

Fat-free food tastes great!

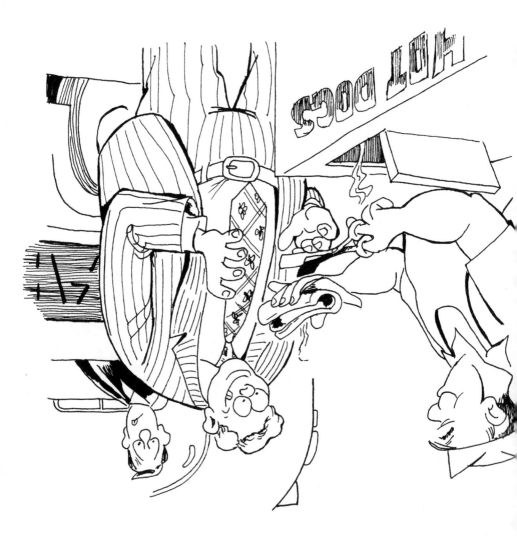

Not to Diet

To Diet

You're starting to have the sleek look of a greyhound—
the bus, not the dog.

Big people can push little people around.

To Diet

You find that you're bigger than everyone else around you.

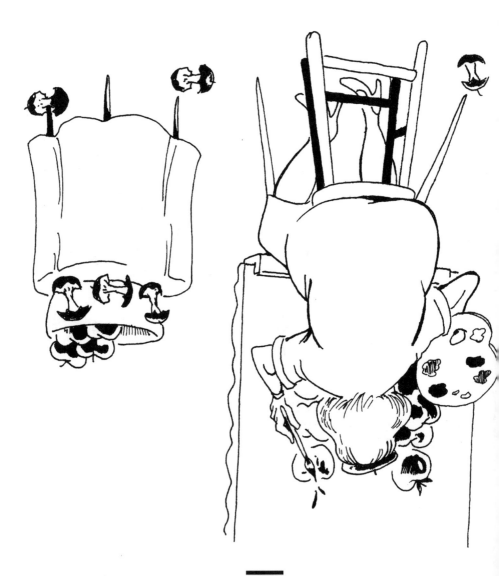

Not to Diet

To Diet

While looking at a still life of a bowl of apples, you find yourself wondering how those apples would taste in a strudel.

You can have your cake and eat it too.

To Diet

Somebody says, "You really take the cake," and you really did.

Your name isn't Jenny Craig.

To Diet

Your name is Jenny Craig.

Not to Diet

true athletes need high-carb, high-energy foods as a power source.
Why should you be any different?

To Diet

ur recipe for trail mix is peanut M&Ms and Hershey chocolate kisses.

Not to Diet

...ding yourself of all that emotional baggage has left you feeling very empty—it's a void that can only be filled by a pizza.

To Diet

ou cleaned out your emotional closet, dumped the garbage of your past, and still didn't lose a pound.

Your feet haven't gained a pound.

To Diet

The last time you bought a size six, you were trying on shoes.

Not to Diet

Evolution clearly favors individuals who can store calories for times of famine.

To Diet

Instead of water, you're retaining chocolate fudge cake
and french fries.

"Everything you see, I owe to spaghetti." —Sophia Loren

To Diet

One can never be too thin.

Not to Diet

To Diet

Thin is not achieved without pain.

Sure—and sometimes it snows in July.

A number of weight-management companies produce full lines
of delicious, low-calorie, frozen dinners.

Not to Diet

That beaded red dress in any size would cost
a year's worth of groceries.

To Diet

There's a size-six beaded red dress you desperately want to buy
for the office Christmas party this year.

Not to Diet

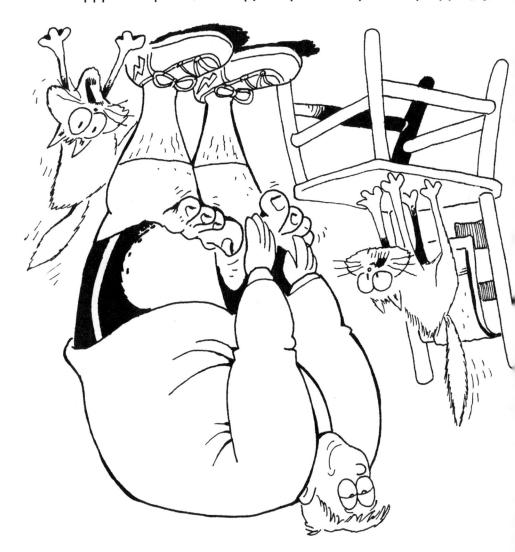

If God had wanted you to play with your toes, he would have put them on your knees where you could reach them.

To Diet

You try to touch your toes but can only reach your knees.

All diets are fishy.

To Diet

You get to eat a lot of fish.

Drinking a shake for breakfast and one for lunch makes
a lot of money for somebody—and it isn't you.

You'll spend a lot less money on groceries.

Not to Diet

It's a great feeling to start each morning with a three-egg omelet and a double rasher of bacon.

To Diet

It's a great feeling to start each morning by weighing yourself
and tracking your weight loss.

Not to Diet

A Miata is a good trade-in on a new Chrysler Minivan.

To Diet

You bought a Miata sports car, but you can't get into it.

Not to Diet

Any man worth having should love you as you are!

To Diet

Your significant other wants you to lose a few pounds.

Not to Diet

Your motto is: Up to the lips and over the gums,
look out stomach, here it comes!

To Diet

Your motto is: A moment on the lips is a lifetime on the hips.

...ce it's *their fault,* why should *you* go on a diet? If the national debt is ...ooning out of proportion, does Congress go on a diet? I don't think so!

Not to Diet

To Diet

Your wardrobe seems to be shrinking at the dry cleaners.

Not to Diet

The only mixed greens that are worth loading up on are twenties, fifties, and hundreds.

On most diets, you can eat all the salad you care to.

Not to Diet

A cabbage diet is about as worthless as the empty head that thought it up.

To Diet

The cabbage diet: All the cabbage you can eat,
fixed any way you like. It's cheap!

Not to Diet

A grapefruit . . . you guessed it . . .
is just as large and worthless as a cabbage.

To Diet

e grapefruit diet: Eat tons of grapefruit and melt the pounds away.

Yes, but we can't all be St. Mary Poppins, can we?

To Diet

Life is easier if you go to bed when you get sleepy, get up early, and go on a diet before you need to.

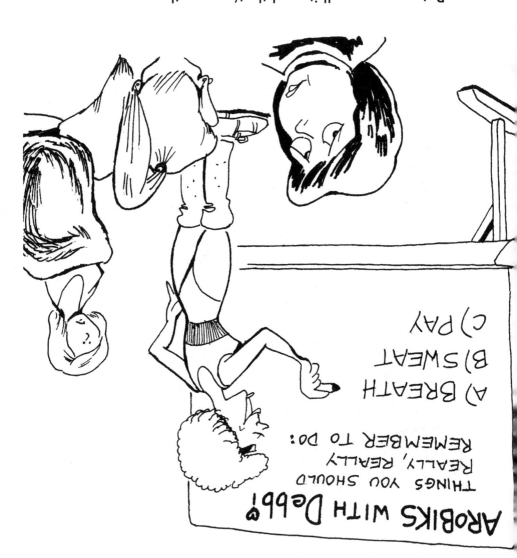

But you can spell it, and that's more than your dizzy-headed instructor can do.

You get winded just saying the word *aerobics.*

Eating is excellent exercise. Just chewing a single mouthful of food burns up five whole calories.

To Diet

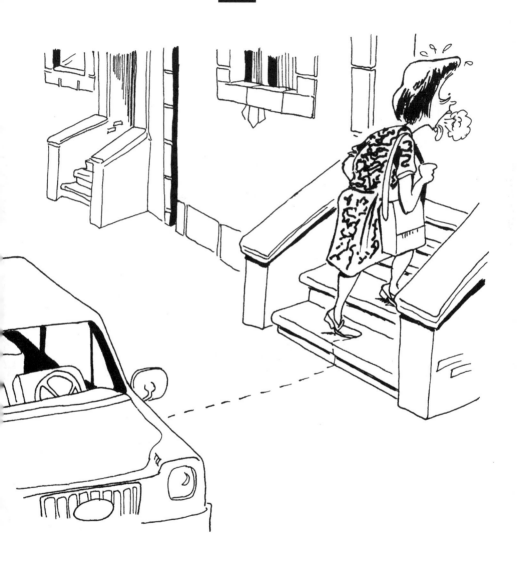

You need to get in shape.

Not to Diet

Light is good in lamps, hearts and touches,
but not in beers, beef or buns.

To Diet

Light is good, light is in.

Not to Diet

Let your mother go on a diet; you're going to the Chinese buffet!

To Diet

Your mother.

Not to Diet

If you made forty million dollars a year just for talking,
you could lose weight too.

Oprah lost 50 pounds on a diet and looks great.

Not to Diet

You never eat more than you can lift.

To Diet

You've been overdoing it at the Food Bar.

God must have loved calories, he made so many of them.

Not to Diet

It's time to cut your caloric intake.

ating is like love. It should be entered into with total abandonment.

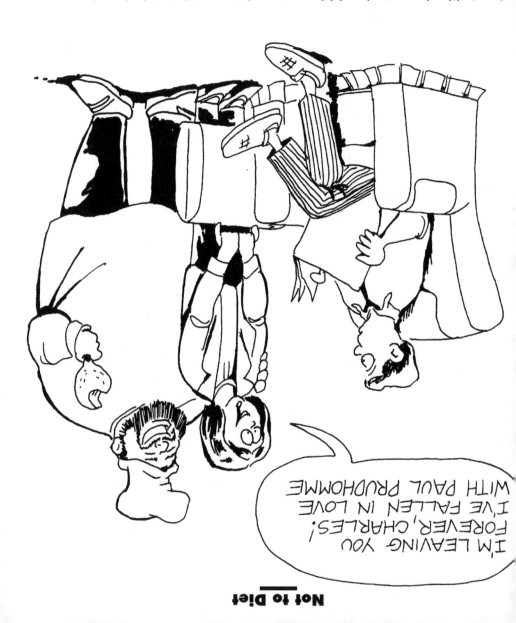

To Diet

You love to eat instead of eat to love.

Not to Diet

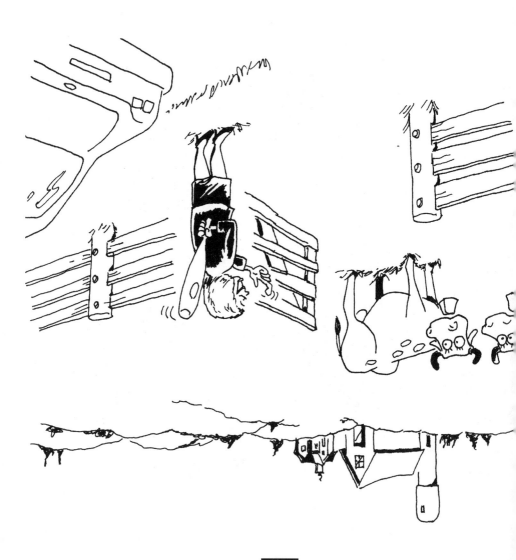

A diet teaches you to eat like a rabbit, live hungry, and develop a craving for anything with chocolate or a face.

To Diet

A diet teaches you to eat better, eat less, and develop new tastes.

Not to Diet

Statistics prove that there is no such thing as a long and happy life if you are starving every minute of it.

SHOOT ME!

To Diet

Statistics prove that keeping your weight down contributes
to a long and happy life.

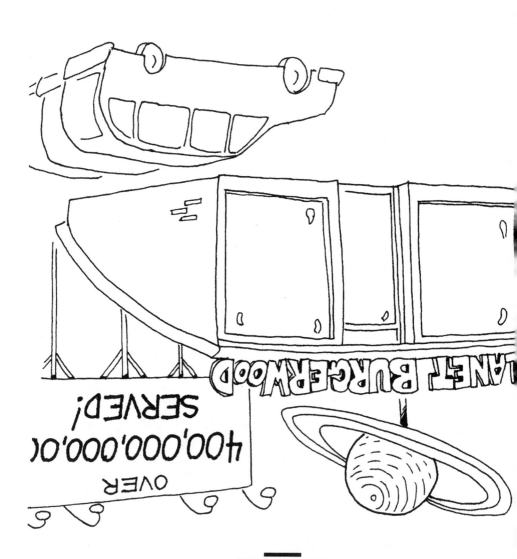

Eating gives you something in common with billions of people.

To Diet

Dieting gives you something in common with millions of people.

Dieting squeezes the heart right out of living.

To Diet

Dieting keeps you from having to squeeze
your heart out to close a zipper.

Not to Diet

After 30 days on a diet, you will definitely notice that you have lost 30 days.

BEFORE

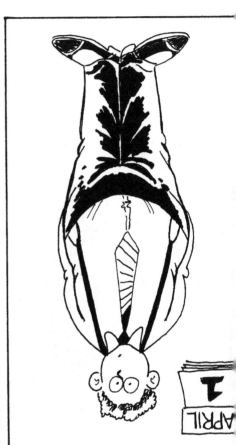

APRIL 1

AFTER

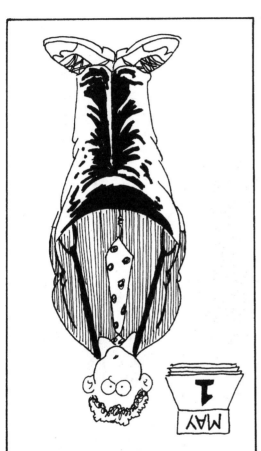

MAY 1

To Diet

After only 30 days on a diet, you will notice a definite loss.

Mirrors are windows to a parallel universe filled with people similar to but larger than you.

<u>To Diet</u>

u look in the mirror in total surprise at the stranger in your clothes.

foods recommended by diets are best when doused with fat-free mayo, sprinkled with wine vinegar, topped with fresh sprouts, then thrown out.

To Diet

The best diet is composed of modest portions of foods
that are good for you and fun to eat.

Face it—there's no life without french fries.

To Diet

Staying on a diet is easy. There are just certain
foods you learn to live without.

People who go around looking at their behinds in store windows are perverts!

Your horizons are expanding backwards.

This Flip-Flop book is part of a series. Look for the others:

50 Good Reasons to Be a Cowboy
50 Good Reasons Not to Be a Cowboy

50 Good Reasons to Have a Cat
50 Good Reasons Not to Have a Cat
(A Cat-Lover's Dilemma)
forthcoming fall 1997

50 Good Reasons to Be a Teacher
50 Good Reasons Not to Be a Teacher
(forthcoming)